Therapy

Gerri C. Borenstein

Franklin Watts
A Division of Scholastic Inc.
New York • Toronto • London • Auckland • Sydney
Mexico City • New Delhi • Hong Kong
Danbury, Connecticut

Dedication

For Jeffrey and Dana, who taught me how to listen

Cover illustration by Peter Cho.
Cover and interior design by Kathleen Santini.

Library of Congress Cataloging-in-Publication Data

Borenstein, Gerri C.
    Therapy / by Gerri C. Borenstein.
        p. cm. — (Life balance)
    Summary: Examines the behaviors or feelings that might lead
    one to seek psychotherapy, what to expect during a counseling
    session, getting the most out of treatment, and knowing when
    it is time to end therapy.
    Includes bibliographical references and index.
    ISBN 0-531-12269-7 (lib. bdg.)   0-531-15585-4 (pbk.)
        1. Adolescent psychotherapy—Juvenile literature. [1. Psycho-
    therapy.] I. Title. II. Series.
    RJ503.B67 2003
    616.89′14′0835—dc21
                                            2003000109

Table of Contents

Mental Health
Matters

Young people today live in a unique time. Opportunities and expectations are higher than ever before. The pressures to keep up, to do better, and to achieve more are hitting you on all fronts—at home, at school, and with your peers. On the one hand, you are fortunate to have all the benefits and advantages of science and technology to make things bigger, better, and faster. On the other hand, there's still no high-tech solution for being happy and successful. That will require a new focus on your mental and physical health. Together, they can provide you with the balance you need to make good decisions without making waves.

Mental health may be something you and your friends have joked about, teased someone else about, or never even thought about. But it's nothing to ignore or laugh about if you're the one struggling to keep a healthy balance in your life. Knowing how and where to go for help with a physical problem is simple. A visit to the family doctor or the school nurse usually solves the problem. Unfortunately, it's not that clear-cut with mental-health problems.

These types of problems may require that you or your family go to a mental-health professional for therapy. Just like going to a dermatologist to clear up your acne or an orthodontist to correct a problem with your teeth, going to a therapist starts with a problem and ends with a solution. What happens in between has a lot to do with who you are and what is happening in your world.

Coping with Life

When you were younger, life may have seemed simpler. You breezed along through most situations with no hassles, no problems, and few conflicts. Stickers and cookies took away the pains and hurts of everyday life, and you had a cozy blanket or a favorite doll to cuddle for comfort. All that really mattered was having a grown-up nearby to make everything better. However, in today's world that is not always possible.

In the first place, blended families are more common than ever, and you may find yourself in the midst of a complicated situation. Your family may have two parents, multiple stepparents, or one parent at home. ("Parent" refers to the adult or adults who are responsible for you and with whom you live.) You or someone you know may live with a grandparent, a relative, or a foster parent. A family may have two houses with stepbrothers and/or sisters and lots of pets or no pets. Try not to fall into the trap of comparing your situation with someone else's—you and your family are the real deal.

Try not to fall into the trap of comparing your situation with someone else's—you and your family are the real deal.

In the second place, you are entering the ping-pong zone called puberty where your body and your brain battle one another and change your appearance, your moods, and your desires. During puberty, special chemicals in your body called hormones start the physical process of changing you from a child into an adult. According to the American Academy of Pediatrics, this can happen anytime between the ages of eight and eighteen. Girls begin to menstruate and develop breasts and pubic hair. They also experience changing body weight and shape. Boys begin to develop mature sexual organs and facial and body hair. They also have to deal with deepening voices and sudden growth spurts.

These physical changes alone can cause self-consciousness, embarrassment, or worry, especially if they start earlier or later than your classmates. Thirteen-year-old Melissa was not at all comfortable with her new body. "Boys stared a lot more and assumed that I was much older than I am. That scared me," she says. "I needed a lot of reassurance from my mom that I was still me, even though I looked a lot different."

Boys experience similar worries. Although twelve-year-old Alex had always been the short one among his group of friends, it never really bothered him until one day, in what seemed like a sudden change, his friends towered over him. Afraid that he would be left behind, Alex started to smoke. "I thought it would make me feel cool but all it did was make me sick," admits Alex. He gave up smoking quickly and instead simply waited it out until his hormones kicked in. Soon, Alex was the same height as most of his friends. Many of these issues and concerns around puberty are temporary as you and your friends catch up with one another. You may feel awkward or uncomfortable during this time, as you come to grips with new feelings and concerns about your self-image.

Puberty Equals Change

According to a report from the surgeon general, the physical changes of puberty are often accompanied by major emotional changes, which can alter the way you feel about yourself and your relationships. These changes can cause periods of stress, feelings of rejection, and maybe even anger as you grow and develop.

Puberty is also the time when you want more freedom, but your parents want more control. You want to go to the school dance; your parents want you to babysit. Maybe they can't stand your clothes, your music, or your attitude. It's also likely that you have more homework and harder tests. As a result, balancing schoolwork and social life is not as easy as it once was.

Good Mental Health

Where and how you see yourself in the surrounding social structure play a big part in how you think, feel, and act—in other words, your mental health. Mental health is a broad term used to describe a state of well-being. It portrays how you feel about yourself (self-esteem) and the world around you. When someone is in good mental health, it generally means that he or she has a positive attitude and sees his or her future in a good way. It may

Resiliency

The characteristics that enable a person to solve problems and make good decisions are often referred to as resilience. The dictionary defines resilience as "having the ability to spring back or recover," but it's much more than that. It is a group of traits that apply to your inner strength and ability to cope with daily life. Being resilient helps explain why some children and adults can overcome the very worst obstacles in their lives—such as severe abuse, poverty, and illness—and go on to become successful and happy, while others cannot.

Not all resilient qualities come naturally to everyone. However, according to leading experts in the field such as researcher Jane Ann Stout of the National Network for Family Resiliency, and physician, speaker, and author Robert Brooks, resilience can be learned. Whether you realize it or not, parents, family members, teachers, and friends all contribute in some way to helping you develop these qualities.

When you think about it, resilience is an integral part of good mental health. Being resilient means you have self-discipline, self-control, and self-esteem. It involves learning skills and behaviors that help you solve problems and make good decisions. It is also about being optimistic and hopeful as well as flexible and realistic, and setting goals and trying to attain them. Having a willingness to try new things and the determination to not give up easily show resiliency, too.

So how do you become a resilient person—the kind who copes with confidence and is able to learn and grow from setbacks, failures, and disappointments? These guidelines can help build your own resilience:

- Stay positive even when a situation is grim.
- Learn how to deal with success and failure.
- Surround yourself with motivated and high-energy friends.
- Seek out those who make you feel special and appreciated.
- Be flexible and compassionate towards others.
- Develop skills, interests, and behaviors that build confidence and happiness.

also refer to strong and healthy relationships at home and with your friends, and confidence about your abilities to get along.

When someone is in good mental health, it generally means that he or she has a positive attitude and sees his or her future in a good way.

When you feel confident and sure of yourself, for example, you're ready to learn at school and to interact with your peers. You can easily handle new situations and challenges because you feel happy and supported. This was not the case with twelve-year-old Ari. When his dad suddenly lost his job, Ari's family had to move in the middle of the school year to a bigger city. "It was so hard for me to break into the cliques in my new school," says Ari, "that I spent a lot more time alone in my room listening to music and visiting chat lines. I felt so out of place that I began skipping school and lying to my parents—until I got caught." Once Ari began therapy, he started to regain his confidence and make new friends.

A good way to gauge your own mental health is to consider how easily you might bounce back from a disappointment, like being cut from a sports team or not being asked to the school dance. When your mental health is good, those small setbacks are easily forgotten and you forge ahead. If you suffer a more serious setback, such as an illness or a death in the family, the chances are greater for developing a problem.

Although you may have read about or know someone who is in therapy, you probably have little idea about the process of therapy and why it works. Often, young people who are experiencing a crisis or a difficult situation are told, "You're going to therapy." All they know is that it doesn't feel like a good thing. The idea of walking into a stranger's office to talk about personal and private things makes many people nervous. Some even feel as if they're being punished for problems that may or may not be their fault. This book will explain what therapy is and how to make it work for you.

Two

Spotting a Problem

According to the United States Department of Health and Human Services, at least one in every five children and adolescents are affected by mental-health problems at any given time. However, an estimated two-thirds of all young people with problems are not getting help. It could be you or someone you know, if the warning signs are not recognized and taken seriously. But that's easier said than done.

First of all, as young people begin to focus more on relationships with friends than with family, it's easy for parents to overlook some early warning signs. Second, many people choose to ignore changes in their own mood or behavior.

That's exactly what sixth grader Sara did for a while. She worried so much about getting all A's that it affected her sleep. "I was tired during the day and couldn't finish my homework. I believed everything would get back to normal if I could just get caught up, but that didn't happen," recalls Sara. "Instead, I had stomachaches and missed a bunch of school." Finally, her teacher spoke to her mom, and together they figured out that something was wrong.

> *Some people mistakenly associate words such as "psycho" or "wacko" with mental health, making it embarrassing and shameful to talk about the subject.*

The third major reason adults and kids ignore emotional problems is the stigma of being labeled a "psycho," "wacko," or "head case." Some people mistakenly associate these words with mental health problems, making it embarrassing and shameful to talk about the subject. Young people and even some adults will do almost anything to avoid admitting they need help for a mental-health problem. But keeping these problems a secret causes many people to suffer needlessly in silence. Eleven-year-old Latisha's friends saw her as outgoing and happy most of the time, but they wondered why she never ate with them in the lunchroom. "I always made excuses, like having to see a teacher or go to the library," she admits, "but most days, I was throwing up in the bathroom." Latisha never expected to end up in a hospital for an eating disorder, but that's how serious her behavior became. "It sure saved me," she tells her friends now. "I learned there is nothing wrong with me physically… My problems are definitely emotional and I'm working hard to be mentally healthy again."

A Healthy Country

President George W. Bush created The President's New Freedom Commission on Mental Health at the University of New Mexico in the spring of 2002. This group hopes to improve the quality of mental-health care by removing some of the misunderstanding, fear, and embarrassment associated with mental health and mental illness. It also hopes to improve the mental health care system. By studying how certain agencies and practitioners in some communities work, members of the commission will try to identify obstacles and barriers to treatment, propose improvements, and make changes that support the goal of making sure that everyone who needs help receives it.

What's Your Problem?

Like Sarah and Latisha, you may have a problem you think you can handle or hide. At first, you may make some bad choices or lapse into a down mood that you cannot shake. You may be worried, stressed out, burned out, or even spaced out. Or you become confused about how to act, or are scared of being left out. When any of those bad feelings stick around too long, they can and do interfere with your life. Even if you confide in no one, your actions will speak louder than your lack of words.

Eventually, symptoms or warning signs may appear and alert someone—a teacher, parent, family friend, clergy member, sibling, or family doctor—that something is wrong. The first step in the therapy process is recognizing when you or a friend are displaying warning signs. When any of these behaviors occur regularly *and* affect your ability to function, then a professional evaluation may be needed. Warning signs include:

- acting disruptively in class
- avoiding usual activities
- talking or thinking in a confused manner
- cutting yourself
- displaying no concept of right or wrong
- eating too much or too little
- being excessively happy
- stressing out
- getting lower grades
- pulling your hair

- not doing your homework
- being moody or irritable
- displaying risky behaviors like using/abusing drugs or alcohol
- demonstrating poor decision-making
- sleeping too much or too little
- talking or thinking about hurting yourself
- being tearful, sad, or blue
- being truant from school
- withdrawing from friends and family

Even when some people are confronted with a problem, however, they may try to talk their way around the issue and convince everyone they are all right. In fact, most big problems do not go away by themselves. They indicate something is wrong physically or emotionally. For example, losing sleep, not eating enough, or crying a lot are unhealthy patterns. These symptoms can get worse and might lead to a more serious medical or emotional problem if they go untreated.

Figuring out what is behind a symptom is not always easy, but there are clues to the puzzle when you look at what is happening in all areas of your life. Problems tend to have a pattern and fall into the following general categories:

Problems with parents/family. Divorce, family violence, illness, death of a family member, and moving are major events that can put young people at risk for developing emotional problems. Power struggles, blended family relationships, and conflicts with a parent or sibling have similar effects.

Problems with self. Low self-esteem, lack of confidence, fear of failure, pressure to excel, fears and worries, and physical illness can prevent you from participating in your usual activities.

Problems with peers. Difficulty making friends, peer pressure, bullying or being bullied, pressure to use alcohol or other substances, social abuse, or exclusion can strain any relationship.

Problems with school. Behaviors that disrupt the classroom or that get you in trouble, truancy, difficulty concentrating, teacher conflicts, test anxiety, fear of failure, excessive competition with peers, learning disabilities, pressures to excel, and being overloaded with activities can interfere with learning.

Stressed Out

Stress is your body's natural physical reaction to situations that may cause you fear and worry. Signs of stress include a fast heartbeat, rapid breathing, high blood pressure, and nervous butterflies in your stomach. Most stress is normal and will disappear once the worrisome activity has passed. For example, you may experience any or all of these physical reactions before going to a party where you don't know many people or when you've done something wrong and have to face your parents. Giving an oral report in front of the class or taking an exam are other big stressors. These feelings usually go away once you engage in the activity you are worried about.

Laugh It Up

According to researchers in all fields of medicine and psychology, laughter can be good for you both physically and mentally. It can reduce stress by lowering your heart rate and making you feel more at ease. Watching a funny video, seeing a movie, or just laughing with friends can work wonders to take your mind and attention off your problems. The Association for Applied and Therapeutic Humor (www.aath.org) is an organization whose sole purpose is to educate people about the benefits of humor and laughter in therapy. Members of this group include psychologists, counselors, nurses, social workers, physicians, business executives, human resource managers, teachers, clergy, hospital clowns, speakers, trainers, and many other specialists. They all support the belief that humor plays an important role in well-being and has therapeutic value.

However, prolonged stress—or stress that lasts longer than it should—can cause many health problems such as heart trouble, ulcers, or headaches. Saying you are "stressed out" may be an overused expression, but it doesn't necessarily mean that you have a serious problem.

Getting Help

The common denominator in all of these problems, from the smallest to the biggest, is the fact that any one of them could compromise your mental health in some way. On the surface, many of these problems may have a simple explanation or cause, but there are two important points to remember: The first is that every problem requires some attention; second, a problem in one part of your life—for example, at school or at home—may easily spill over into other parts.

After Marco's parents split up, his grades went down. Marco's dad thought he was just goofing off, so he was on his case a lot. "I didn't want to be treated like a baby," admitted Marco, "so I never told anyone how much I missed my mom. One night, I raided the liquor cabinet. I didn't care about my homework, myself, or my dad's disapproval. I was drinking a few times a week until my dad finally noticed what was going on." Fortunately, Marco and his family got help, and all the problems associated with the divorce are finally out in the open.

Sometimes you can resolve a problem by yourself or with the help of a trusted adult. But if and when that is not possible, mental-health professionals are good at spotting a problem and relating it to your symptoms. Even if you or your family can make the connection between a symptom and your problem, you may want the help of a therapist so you can cope better with the problem or solve it.

How well you cope with the challenging twists and turns in your life will depend somewhat on the combination of three factors: your personality, your individual experiences, and your support system. Every life event, big or small—from going to school, taking a test, giving a speech, moving away, to dealing with an illness—can be difficult at times. Never assume that you "should" be able to handle something difficult all by yourself. Be sure to give yourself a break

Never assume that you "should" be able to handle something difficult all by yourself.

when the going gets tough. If you take the same positive approach with your mental health as you do with your physical health, you should consider seeing a therapist if you have an emotional problem. Being in top mental form is to your advantage, so don't say "no way" when a parent or other adult suggests therapy.

Three

Choosing a
Therapist

With so many options and resources available, it is easy to get lost and overwhelmed during the search for a therapist. Often, referrals will come from other parents, teachers, school counselors, or family doctors. When someone makes a referral, it means they provide the name of a therapist they know or have heard good things about. Tell your parents if you would prefer to see a male or female therapist, and explain why it matters. Most agencies or group practices will try to meet your request if at all possible.

The period of time before you actually get an appointment to see the therapist

Questions and Answers

Below are some common questions young people have before entering therapy.

1. "Why am I going? There's nothing wrong with me."
   You're right about that. There's nothing wrong with being who you are. But there may be something troublesome about how you behave, think, or feel.

2. "My parents are crazy. Why don't they get therapy?"
   Sometimes problems are reactions to things parents do, such as getting a divorce, remarrying, or moving, so it's natural to blame them. Therapists are trained to hear both sides—yours and your parents—before discussing a plan of action.

3. "What's in it for me?"
   Therapy can help you feel happier and healthier when problems get in the way.

4. "How long will therapy take?"
   There's no quick fix to most problems, so don't

worry if your therapist doesn't give you an exact timetable. Concentrate on your goal to be healthier and happier.

5. "What if I dislike the therapist right away?"
First, ask yourself what you don't like about the person, and be sure you're being fair. If it's something superficial, such as the way he or she looks or dresses, you may have to try to get over it and give him or her a chance. If it's something else that makes you feel uncomfortable, talk it over with your family after the session.

6. "Will the therapist like me?"
Therapists don't generally talk about their feelings. They are trained to be objective and neutral when they counsel others.

7. "What if I don't know what to say?"
Don't worry. The therapist will ask, "Do you know why you're here?" or "What did your mom or dad tell you about coming here?" You can tell

Questions and Answers
(continued)

him or her why *you* think you're there. Giving some background about yourself and the problem will be easier than you think.

8. "Will I get in trouble if I say bad things?"
   No. Therapy is not about punishment. Therapy helps you avoid getting in trouble.

9. "How can I talk about my parents if they're sitting right there?"
   Therapists know that this will be a concern for young people, so they won't put you on the spot. Remember that you are there to talk openly about problems, whether you meet alone with the therapist or with your family.

10. "Will the therapist know what I'm thinking?"
    Mental-health professionals have studied behavior so they can help you understand yours. But they cannot and do not read minds any more than you can.

11. "What if I cry?"
Crying is a fine way to express yourself.

12. "What if I get angry?"
Therapists expect anything and everything, so speak up and speak out.

13. "Will the therapist try to give me drugs?"
Once a diagnosis is made, medication may be prescribed. Be assured that if and when that becomes necessary, you will understand why and how it will help, and you will be involved in the decision about whether or not to take it.

14. "Is the office private, or will there be other people around?"
It will definitely be private. The waiting area may have a receptionist or other office employees nearby, but once you enter the therapist's own office, no one but you (and possibly your family) will be there.

will vary from place to place. Unless it's an emergency (in which case you will be seen right away), the waiting time may be anywhere from a few days to a few weeks. That time can be hard on you and your family. You may worry more about your problem or become more nervous about what it will be like seeing the therapist. You may even feel like your parents or teachers are watching you more carefully during that time. Keep busy and be as active as possible until the day of your appointment.

Where you live may also determine which mental-health services or professionals are available. In big cities, for instance, there are multiple choices of practitioners and agencies. In smaller or more rural communities, the options may be fewer, and your family will have less choice in the matter. Most therapists charge for each session or appointment. Part of their fee may be covered by health insurance. Adults may receive health insurance where they work, or it can be bought privately or be provided by the government. Generally, though, insurance is used to help pay a portion of the cost of medical exams, tests, treatment, and medication—and it may also cover therapy.

The therapist's office may be in your school, a local clinic, a social-service agency, or a private office. If you have to stay overnight or live in a facility for a period of time, that is called an inpatient or residential setting. Remember, where you live, the type of problem you have, and who is available to see you may all determine where you go for therapy and who your therapist will be.

Get the Scoop on the Therapist

Mental-health practitioners may call themselves therapists, psychotherapists, doctors, or counselors. For the most part, it's a matter of professional training and personal preference. Since most young people are more familiar with the word *counselor,* lots of practitioners prefer to use that term. On the other hand, psychiatrists, who are medical doctors, sometimes prefer to use the more traditional term of *psychotherapist* or doctor. Although therapists tend to get put in the same general catagory, this varied group of mental-health practitioners differs greatly when it comes to level of education, training, and experience.

A *guidance counselor* is a person who handles everything from curriculum to social problems in school. He or she may often be the one to recommend outside therapy for a problem. A college degree is required.

A *social worker* is a professional trained to provide social services and counseling to individuals, families, and groups. A college degree plus a graduate degree is required.

A *licensed clinical social worker* (LCSW) is a mental-health professional with advanced training in social services and counseling for individuals, families, and groups. A college degree and graduate program, plus additional hours of psychotherapy experience and training, are required. He or she must also meet state testing and experience requirements before being licensed.

A *school psychologist* is a mental-health professional who works in schools. He or she can provide therapy but is also trained to perform psychological assessment tests. A college degree plus advanced training is required.

A *psychologist* or clinical psychologist is a mental-health professional trained to do psychological assessment tests, psychotherapy, and/or psychological research. A college degree and a graduate degree, plus a certain number of hours supervised by an experienced professional, are required. If he or she has completed doctoral training, then the psychologist will be called "doctor" and is identified by the degrees Ph.D. or Psy.D. A psychologist is licensed by the state. (In the state of New Mexico, he or she may also qualify to prescribe certain medications.)

A *psychiatrist* is a licensed medical doctor (M.D.) with advanced training in evaluating and treating medical and mental, emotional, or behavioral disorders. Psychiatrists are the only mental-health professionals who can prescribe medication in all states. A college degree and a medical degree, plus internship and residency training in psychiatry and psychotherapy, are required. A psychiatrist must be licensed by the state in which he or she practices.

Pastoral counselors, rabbis, and **mental-health workers** are other possible counselors.

Your parents will likely pay close attention to a therapist's education and training, but the most important consideration for *you* is making a positive connection with the therapist. While it's a good idea to see someone who has experience working with young people and with similar problems to yours, keep an open mind about the therapist's background when you make the final decision about which therapist is best for you. Look for qualities and experience that put you at ease.

> *The most important consideration for* **you** *is making a positive connection with the therapist. Look for qualities and experience that put you at ease.*

The Right Choice

Many young people do not always have a choice about starting therapy. But that doesn't mean you don't have any rights or choices once you start. Your rights include:

- The right to feel safe. At no time in therapy should you feel threatened or scared.

Learn the Lingo

Mental-health professionals speak a language all their own. The following are some words and clinical terms associated with therapy:

- *Psychotherapy*—also called therapy, or counseling—is referred to as the "talking cure" because talking and listening are the major elements of the process.
- *Behavior therapy* is an approach used to change current behavior rather than to examine feelings.
- *Clients/patients* refers to you or anyone else who is using therapy to work through problems.
- *Issues* are the problems or concerns discussed in therapy.
- *Sessions* are therapy appointments.
- *Mood* is a continuous and dominant emotion that influences your perception of the world.
- *Psychotropic drugs*, such as antidepressants, tranquilizers, and mood stabilizers, are sometimes prescribed by a physician to help restore your mental well-being.
- *Termination* means you and your therapist mutually agree to stop therapy.

- The *therapeutic relationship* is a unique working relationship that develops between you and your therapist. This relationship is based on your trust in him or her. Once that's established, you can feel comfortable to reveal secrets and true feelings without embarrassment, fear, or shame. Although you may feel very close to your therapist, the relationship is different from one you might have with any other health professional. Therapists do not share much personal information with you nor do they socialize with you outside of therapy.

- *Confidentiality* means that what you share in therapy will be between just you and your therapist, unless it threatens your personal safety or that of someone else's. This complicated privilege is different for people under the age of eighteen because they are not yet legally responsible for themselves. That means your parents have a legal right to get information about your therapy, but in most cases, your therapist will reach a working agreement with you and your family about what is to remain private. Be sure to have a discussion about this important issue when you begin your therapy.

- The right to know what is confidential. Although there is no legal right to privacy for people under the age of eighteen, your therapist and parents will agree on acceptable professional guidelines to keep private the information you share unless it threatens your personal safety or the safety of someone else.
- The right to tell no one or anyone you choose about your therapy. It's your personal decision if and when to tell.
- The right to talk about anything you want. Therapy is the time and place to discuss whatever is on your mind.
- The right to answer or not answer questions. No one can force you to answer if you are not ready or willing to answer.
- The right to disagree. Your opinions and thoughts always matter during therapy.
- The right to feel the way you do. You and your emotions are unique to you.
- The right to say no to something you are unsure of or to something that makes you feel uncomfortable. You should not agree to do anything that you have questions about regarding your therapy.
- The right to be treated with respect. At no time should your therapist make you feel bad, stupid, or foolish about something you say or do.

- The right to schedule appointments so you won't miss a lot of school or after-school activities. Work with your parents and therapist on this whenever possible.

Now that you have chosen the kind of therapy situation that feels right for you, think about what you really want to get out of therapy. How will you explain what is bothering you? What do you want to change in your life? What role do you want your family to play? Therapy is hard work, and you will need to do a lot of it on your own. Let's get started.

Four

The First Session

The first meeting with a therapist is your opportunity to check each other out. In a way, it's no different than walking into class on the first day of a new school year. You are hoping the teacher's easygoing and friendly. Your teacher hopes you are an eager student. For both of you, that first meeting will set the tone for what will follow. Making it work will depend on both of you.

In the beginning, many young people are nervous, angry, or reluctant to go to therapy. Therapists understand this, so they will do everything they can to put you at ease and make you feel comfortable. Phyllis DiLea, a social worker from

Utica, New York, explains her approach this way. "A therapist is like the coach of a team," she explains. "I describe the plays and design a practice, but only you—the player—can make it work." Your therapist will work *with* you and *for* you but is only an advisor, confidante, and mentor. He or she can't make change happen without your help.

Another psychologist, who works in private practice, uses the first session as an opportunity to convince young people that their stories will be safe with her. She knows they talk to their friends, parents talk to teachers, and teachers talk to parents, so explaining privacy to her clients is important. She knows that if she fails to gain her client's trust, therapy will not succeed.

Just the Facts

The first appointment is basically an evaluation. It is likely that a family member will take you and be part of it. You may all meet together for a while before you meet alone with the therapist, or you may meet alone first and then together. It's important for a parent to be there at some point to provide the necessary background information about your medical, social, and family history. But if you feel strongly about it one way or another, be sure to say so.

"A therapist is like the coach of a team... I describe the plays and design a practice, but only you—the player—can make it work."

The therapist will ask a lot of questions in order to gather information about what your life is like at home, at school, and with your friends. Those details will help the therapist get a handle on the problem. He or she might ask you to describe your friends, hobbies, and school activities. The therapist may even ask about your eating and sleeping habits and personal hygiene. Some questions may seem stupid or silly, but the therapist is trying to get an accurate picture of what you're like. Other problem-related questions include:

- How do you feel about coming to therapy?
- How would you describe the problem?
- How long have you had the problem?
- Did anything make the problem worse?

- When and how was it noticed?
- Do you know what caused the problem?
- Have you tried to fix the problem?
- If so, what worked and what did not?

Because you and your parents may see a problem differently, it's important for the therapist to hear both sides, as was the case with twelve-year-old Elizabeth and her mom. Elizabeth felt as though her mom was always watching her and snooping around, hoping to catch her doing something wrong. Her mom, on the other hand, didn't know many of Elizabeth's new friends, nor was she comfortable with her daughter's sudden secrecy about her social plans. When all communication between them practically stopped, her mom read Elizabeth's diary, which confirmed her worst fears.

During their first session, the therapist made it clear that she was there to help both of them deal with the situation. She explains, "I try to show kids right away that I'm not just taking their parent's side. I want kids to feel like they own part of the solution and are not just getting blamed for a problem."

Through therapy, Elizabeth and her mom established new boundaries and worked on regaining each other's trust. Elizabeth needed to acknowledge that being at parties where drinking was involved and hanging out with older kids was a legitimate risk for her, and that her mother had a right to be concerned. In turn, the therapist was able to get Elizabeth's mom to admit she was wrong to invade her daughter's privacy by reading her diary.

In some cases, the therapist may suggest consulting with another type of physician or therapist. A consult means that the therapist needs to clarify something, and he or she wants a more appropriately trained doctor or other professional to assist in the process. Your therapist might also want you to have blood tests, X-rays, or special assessments such as speech and language evaluations. Usually, this happens when a therapist suspects there may be an underlying medical or biological cause to your problem(s).

The therapist may also want to meet with your teacher, the social worker, or the guidance counselor at school. If the therapist feels that such meetings will be helpful to you, don't hesitate to agree. When Brent began seeing a counselor, he and his teacher were not on the best of terms. He often came to class late and disrupted the lessons. He showed a lack of concern for the other kids who made it back on time after lunch. When the teacher asked him to sit up front one day, he refused. Instead of going to the principal's office as his teacher asked, Brent kicked over a chair.

When he began counseling, one of the first things the therapist did was to set up a meeting at his school. Anger management was a huge problem for Brent, and his therapist wanted the support of his school to help Brent understand it and learn positive ways to control it. Recommending a consultation doesn't mean that your therapist doesn't like you or that he or she thinks you are too far gone to help. It just means your therapist is doing a thorough job.

Continuing Therapy

At the end of the first or the first few meetings, the therapist will ask you and/or your parents about whether or not you feel that you would like to continue working together. He or she may have presented you with some type of treatment plan, which is an outline of how the therapist thinks you can be helped. Neither you nor your family is obligated to say yes on the spot. You may want to talk things over in private before agreeing to go back. The important thing is to make sure you feel you can work with that person.

More than anything else, trust yourself. Pay attention to the vibes between you and the therapist during those first sessions. You should be able to answer yes to the following questions:

- Did you feel comfortable?
- Did the therapist explain what therapy is all about?
- Did you both clarify why you are in therapy?
- Did the room feel inviting and private?
- Did the therapist listen to what you had to say?
- Did the therapist appear interested and concerned?
- Did you feel all right about agreeing to go back again?

If the connection was positive, you're headed in the right direction. It's time to learn and explore what's going on in your life. Don't lose sight of the fact that therapy is a smart choice, even if, at first, it was not *your* choice. In the next chapter, we'll explain what happens once you begin therapy.

Five

Giving Therapy a Try

Agreeing to start therapy is a positive move. It means you're willing to take an important step toward conquering obstacles and managing your life. The best way to begin is simple: Start talking and keep listening.

The Goals of Therapy

Therapy involves three phases: (1) figuring out where a problem came from, (2) fixing a problem, and (3) learning how to avoid future problems. In the first phase, you and your therapist will set up some ground rules about confidentiality as well as how many sessions you will have and how often you will meet. You will focus mainly on developing a relationship with one another during the first few meetings. In the second phase, the focus is on expressing your feelings about the problems in your life. Your therapist will guide you in discussions about what's been happening to make you feel the way you do. He or she will encourage you to talk about the issues that are affecting school, friends, and family. The third phase focuses on finding a solution.

Therapists are trained to use a variety of approaches or techniques in order to get the right fit for each person and his or her problem. Approaches can change during therapy or even during a session, depending on what's going on. The most important thing is that you are listened to and everyone communicates well. Depending on your personality and your problem, your therapist will use one or more of the following approaches to help you.

Individual psychotherapy/therapy

Individual psychotherapy is one-to-one. This means that just you and a therapist will meet on a regular basis to work out your problems. The therapist will ask questions and listen to your answers in order to make a connection between a problem and past events. Over time, you will share your feelings about the situation and will be guided toward a greater understanding of yourself. Even though one or both of your parents may meet with you on occasion, this method of talk therapy is usually between you and the therapist.

Family therapy

Family therapy takes place with your family. This means you and some or all of your family will meet together with a therapist to resolve both individual and family matters. The primary goal is to improve communication among family members and learn effective techniques to help solve problems.

Group therapy

Group therapy involves working together with other people who have similar problems. This means you will meet together as a group with one or more therapists as you learn from your peers how to resolve your own problems. Young people often find it easier to open up to others their age and can often learn a lot from one another.

Behavior therapy or cognitive-behavior therapy

Behavior therapy, sometimes called cognitive-behavior therapy, can be one-on-one or with family members. This approach focuses more on changing behavior than it does on talking. You and the therapist will identify the negative aspects of the way you think and act and will try to turn that into positive thinking and acting.

Tired of Talking

Some problems can be resolved in ways other than talking. Relaxation techniques such as yoga, meditation, and deep breathing are easily learned and practiced at home or at school. Using these techniques on a regular basis can help you to refocus your energy and gain control of your emotions. They are a great way to "chill out" quietly, so you can use them alone or in a group situation.

Other therapies employ art and music to help you express yourself more easily. You can paint, draw, sculpt with clay, or try anything else artistic that your imagination allows. You can also listen to music, play an instrument, or even compose a song. The best thing about art and music therapy is that they require no artistic ability or skill—just a willingness to try.

Take It Slow

No one will expect you to jump right in with the hard stuff. If something is difficult to talk about or too painful to relive, you can take your time before opening up. When and how you do that is your call. To help you open up, the therapist may ask you to draw pictures, play with action figures or dolls, or make up a story to explain a problem or concern. Some therapists even use printouts that describe emotions in easy-to-understand language or that show multiple faces, which can help you better describe how you are feeling that day.

You'll also have the chance to talk about the kinds of things you do for fun. If you're interested in books, videos, or music, you can share what you like and dislike. That's an easy way to show off different sides of your personality. Some therapists may take walks, play video or board games, or do research on the Internet with you. You may even get to share some of your writing from a diary or work on your homework together.

As you begin to trust the therapist more, talking to him or her will get easier. Anna remembers how she felt when she first started therapy. "I was scared at first to tell why I didn't like to eat. But my therapist never rushed me, and waited until I was ready." Thomas felt the same way. At first he thought he was in trouble when his doctor recommended medicine, until she took the time to explain the chemistry behind Thomas's depression. "Now I know it's not my fault and I didn't do anything to deserve it."

Finding Solutions

The third phase of therapy focuses on finding solutions. If you are having test anxiety, for instance, you will practice techniques that can help you overcome it. For example, your therapist may set a timer and have you take a practice

Therapy Works

The more you put into your therapy the more you will get out of it. It's no different than tackling a new subject or sport. So give it your best shot from the start by actively participating and following some of these suggestions:

- Show up   *Your session is reserved just for you.*

- Be honest   *Share what you think, feel, and fear.*

- Build a rapport   *Talk and listen to establish trust.*

- Do the work   *Practice exercises, try techniques, or follow suggestions to help achieve your goals.*

- Give feedback   *Say what you like and don't like about your progress in therapy.*

- Measure your success   *Do you feel better, happier, and more satisfied?*

- Take control   *Communicate, connect, and cope with confidence.*

test in the office. By observing you, your therapist can help identify some of the difficulties you may be having. Together, you will then work on implementing effective changes to relieve your anxiety.

If you're seeing a therapist for behavioral problems, such as making angry or aggressive outbursts, the approach will be similar. You may be asked to keep a journal that details what you were doing before an outburst occurred and how you felt after it happened. Once you are able to do that, it's possible to adapt or modify your behavior for the better.

In family therapy, conflict and power struggles over rules, dress, homework, and curfew are often the focus. To improve communication and bring about positive changes, role-playing is often used. This is where you get to act out the part of the parent and your parent plays you. By changing sides in a power struggle, you and your parents may *both* become more open to compromise in order to reach a solution.

Clinical psychologist and family therapist Tom Scott, Ph.D., aims for three A's when he counsels young people and their families: a good *attitude*, a common *agenda*, and appropriate *action*. He believes that all parties must agree to try to improve a situation or to resolve a conflict. They must share a common agenda on what it is they want to change. And, they both need to act in ways that make change possible.

Family therapist Tom Scott, Ph.D., aims for three A's when he counsels young people and their families: a good attitude, a common agenda, and appropriate action.

What If...

... I start to like the therapist too much and wish he or she were my parent? It's all right to let your therapist know how you feel. If someone is supportive and kind to you, it's natural to feel this way. You may even feel this way about a friend's parent, a teacher, or a coach.

... I get upset when my therapist goes away? If you've been seeing him or her regularly, you may find yourself depending on that special time to talk things out. Or you may be worried that the therapist won't come back. Give it time. Soon you will feel more secure.

... I sometimes feel worse talking about things? Talking openly about painful events in your life is a sign you are ready to face them. You may feel sadder as you retell the incident, or relive it, but that's how you learn to deal with bad experiences.

... my friends don't like me after they find out I am in therapy? Remember, it's your call on how or when to tell a friend. But if he or she drops you, was this person really your friend?

... therapy is boring and stupid one day and great the next? No activity—including therapy—is exciting or meaningful all the time.

... I want to bring my therapist a gift? Generally, this is not done without first discussing it with your therapist. Once he or she says it's all right, consider giving something you've made yourself or paid for with money you earned.

... I want to know about my therapist's kids? It's all right to ask. But don't forget, you're there to talk about you and your family, not the therapist's.

Blame Doesn't Solve Problems

Any kind of turmoil in your life can change your mental and physical health; some turmoil you create yourself, and some you do not. For instance, an illness or death in the family causes a great deal of stress. Divorce and remarriage can create more conflict and problems. You may feel ignored by an absentee parent or find it hard to relate to the parent you're with. Problems like these are easily blamed on your parents, but blaming only makes matters worse. In these situations, a therapist can be the adult who intervenes on your behalf. He or she can take the lead as you work on improving things at home.

In other situations, blaming someone or something else for the way you feel or behave *is* part of the problem. Your therapist will help you look inward to explain the cause and effect of your actions in these situations. Samantha's story explains this more clearly. She was a happy and popular seventh-grader until her best friend dumped her for a boyfriend. "Suddenly I felt like a total geek and a loser," she said. "My ex-best friend's popularity made me so jealous I started making up stories about her and spreading them around school."

It didn't take long for that tactic to backfire. Before long, Samantha became isolated from her friends. She finally talked to her mom, who helped her get into therapy. "It's taken a while," admits Samantha, "but my therapist helped me understand that my low self-esteem was the problem—not my friend's behavior."

Matt was an amazing athlete and a decent student, but once he hit middle school, he began to have trouble with math. He blamed himself for "not getting it." When some low test scores threw him for a loop, Matt's guidance counselor suspected a learning problem. With testing and counseling, Matt is now doing fine. "It wasn't easy at first, but now I know that my learning disabilities don't mean I'm stupid."

One of the best parts of therapy is having the undivided attention, encouragement, and support of your therapist. Your personal time in therapy may be the one and only place where you are free to focus on yourself without feeling selfish. You may actually reach a stage where you like going to therapy. As you become more tuned into yourself and more connected to the therapist, you may have some new feelings and questions to think about. Get ready for them.

It's hard to know how long therapy will take but once you begin to feel like yourself (or even a better self!) again, you are ready to move on. You may have had several therapists, different medications, and family involvement. No matter how much therapy you have or what it involves, you'll eventually reach your goal—and be ready to jump back into life.

Six

Keeping the
Balance

Being healthy for thirteen-year-old Katie means being able to cope better. There was a time when Katie and her family fought so much that she ran away. When the school notified her parents, they were frantic. They had no idea how much their yelling affected her. Running away got their attention, but family therapy got them communicating. "Therapy helped me understand my weird parents," jokes Katie. "Now we laugh a lot more and yell a lot less."

It was like that for Sam, too. He was strong-willed and frequently pushed the limits with his parents. At twelve, he thought he should be allowed to do whatever he wanted. "I still flip out when my parents say no," he admits, "but at least they say 'yes' once in a while, too." Sam believes that therapy helped bring about this change.

When Jessica ended up in the school counselor's office for cheating on an exam, she was nearly hysterical. "Telling my dad was the hardest of all because he expected so much from me," says eleven-year-old Jessica. "I felt like a disappointment to him since I wasn't always the best student." Once she got into therapy, Jessica's sense of self-worth began to change for the better. She started piano lessons and was surprised to discover how much she loved it. Her new interest and talent gave her confidence that carried over to her schoolwork. Now she and her dad are more realistic about their expectations.

Saying Good-bye

Feeling better and happier usually marks the beginning of the end of therapy. If you make it this far, you'll be ready for the final phase: letting go. This is the time when you and your therapist are on the same wavelength, and you both agree that you're ready to terminate treatment. This realization happens gradually but is no surprise when it emerges. There are plenty of indicators along the way.

First of all, your symptoms are gone, and there are no lingering signs of a problem. Doing well in your normal activities comes more easily now that you feel good about yourself. Another positive sign is when you and your therapist have less to talk about, or you start wanting to cancel sessions because you have things that are more fun to do.

Why, then, do you feel bad about saying good-bye? You and your therapist have shared a unique relationship. He or she has been a mentor, advisor, role model, or friend. You also got used to seeing this person on a regular basis. He or she has helped you understand your problems by putting you first and appreciating your strengths. In fact, your therapist helped you succeed. It's only natural you should feel sad about losing someone who has played an important role in your well-being. Don't worry too much if you have those feelings. Lots of people in therapy have them.

You may wonder if you'll ever talk to the therapist again. It is common practice to call a therapist to share some good news once you leave. And, lots of times, you may go back to your therapist for a "tune-up." That means returning for just a few visits to get clarification about something or to reconnect about a past problem. It doesn't necessarily mean that you will begin the therapy

Help Yourself to Health

An overall healthy lifestyle is important for everyone—young and old—throughout their lifetime. Many physical illnesses, such as obesity, diabetes, and heart disease, can have a direct impact on your emotional well being, so it's important to try and reduce your chances of developing these illnesses. There are many positive things you can do to stay healthy, including avoiding drugs, alchohol, and cigarettes; getting the proper nutrition; the right amount of sleep; and daily amounts of exercise. When it comes to exercise, don't overdo it. Just do something that you enjoy. Get creative and be willing to experiment with new or different forms of exercise when you and/or the weather change.

- *Exercise*   Physical activity is an ideal stress reliever.

- *Eat right*   A healthy diet helps you sleep well and think better.

- *Laugh*   A sense of humor eases tension and can help you feel comfortable in difficult situations.

- *Talk to friends*   Share the highs and lows with your pals. Their support is priceless.

- *Help others*   Get involved at school or in the community. It makes you feel good and keeps you connected.

- *Keep a journal*   Vent your feelings in private. It can help you clarify things.

process all over again. Your therapist keeps your records in a safe place once therapy ends, but they are available for him or her to review again if you need to return.

Moving On

Imagine yourself a few years from now when you're in high school or about to go off to college or to start a job. It will take a lot of hard work and determination to get there. New challenges and opportunities will always be part of your future, and to stay focused and balanced will require constant attention to your mental and physical health. Now that you understand more about what therapy is and what it isn't, you will be more open to getting help along the way if things ever become too hard to handle.

Therapy can and does help many people get to a good place in their life, but one of the most important lessons to take away from therapy is the realization that the therapist cannot fix everything. In real life, some problems have no real solutions. Sometimes it's simply a

One of the most important lessons to take away from therapy is the realization that the therapist cannot fix everything. In real life, some problems have no real solutions.

matter of learning how to live with a difficulty or how to make the best of a bad situation.

Eleven-year-old Luis knew nothing could bring back his dad, who recently died of cancer. Through group therapy he met other kids who had also lost a parent. "I got control of how I felt even though I couldn't control what happened to me. That helped me and the other kids get better faster." Remember that, in therapy, you help yourself as much as your therapist helps you. That fact alone is one of the best reasons for being in therapy.

So, how can you maintain balance once you say goodbye to the therapist? Doing all the things required to stay physically healthy is one way. But keeping tabs on your emotions is another. That means you won't avoid or ignore problems if and when they arise. It is better to resolve a problem while it is still small, rather than wait for it to snowball into something larger. Telling someone if and when you have a problem should be a lot easier in the future. Having support and guidance is one of the best ways to get through a bad time.

And finally, put away the put-downs. Mental-health problems may affect anyone at any time—even you. If you remember nothing else about therapy, keep in mind that it is all about communication, coping, and confidence. And there's nothing wrong with that.

Glossary

acting out: self-abusive, aggressive, and/or disruptive behavior

assessment: see *evaluation*

behavioral disorder: acting inappropriately for one's age over an extended period of time and in a socially unaccept-able way

chronic: lasting a long time or recurring

community-based services: clinics or practices that are part of the community

consult: when your therapist recommends that you see another professional to clarify something or to help treat you evaluation: a process conducted by mental-health professionals that results in an opinion about a child's mental or emotional capacity, and may include recommendations about treatment or placement

inpatient: services received while residing in the hospital or a residential facility

mental health: a broad term that describes a state of emotional well-being

mental illness: a disorder or severe emotional problem

outpatient: services received in an office or clinic setting

psychotherapy: known as the "talking cure" because talking and listening are the major parts of this type of therapy

referral: when an individual is pointed in the direction of a specific person or place for treatment

stigma: when something feels like a disgrace, shame, or embarrassment

stress: a physical reaction brought on by a difficulty, pressure, or worry stressor: events or concerns that cause stress

symptom: any sign or indication of a problem or illness

therapeutic: having healing or curative qualities

withdrawing behavior: showing reduced interest in or
contact with other people

Further Resources

Books

Canfield, Jack. *Chicken Soup for the Teenage Soul III: More Stories of Life, Love, and Learning.* Deerfield Beach, FL: Health Communications, 2000.
Real life stories about life, love, and learning from teens.

Canfield, Jack. *Chicken Soup for the Teenage Soul on Tough Stuff: Stories of Tough Times and Lessons Learned.* Deerfield Beach, FL: Health Communications, 2001.
Real life stories about teens' experiences with stress, pressures, and depression. Also tackles issues such as school violence, suicide, and abuse.

Gordon, Sol. *When Living Hurts: For Teenagers and Young Adults.* New York: Union of American Hebrew Congregations, 1994.
This book is addressed to teenagers who may be feeling depressed or suicidal, or who want to help someone else who is troubled. Topics discussed include worries about sex and love, religion, relationships with parents, and purpose in life. A list of crisis intervention and suicide prevention hot lines around the country is included.

Gordon, Sol. *A Friend in Need: How to Help When Times Are Tough.* Amherst, NY: Prometheus Books, 2000.
This book can help you to help a friend during difficult times. It contains easy-to-follow advice on what to say and do when friends are coping with obstacles such as an abusive relationship, illness, or a death in the family.

Kaufman, Gershen, Lev Raphael, and Pamela Espeland. *Stick Up for Yourself: Every Kid's Guide to Personal Power & Positive Self-Esteem.* Minneapolis, MN: Free Spirit Publishing, 1999.
This award-winning book explains self-esteem and why you need it. It offers lots of advice about how to deal with problems, how to make responsible choices, and how each of us can develop personal power.

Mirriam-Goldberg, Caryn. *Write Where You Are: How to Use Writing to Make Sense of Your Life.* Minneapolis, MN: Free Spirit Publishing, 1999.
Learn a creative way to express yourself. This book provides lots of good advice and specific writing exercises to help understand what's happening in your life as well as your emotions about difficult topics.

Pamphlets and fact sheets

Federation of Families for Children's Mental Health. *Blamed and Ashamed.*

This unique monograph documents the treatment experiences of youth with co-occurring mental health and substance abuse disorders from the perspective of youth and their families. It was made possible by support from the U.S. Substance Abuse and Mental Health Services Administration (SAMHSA). It is available, for a small postage & handling fee, from the Federation of Families for Children's Mental Health, 1101 King Street, Suite 420, Alexandria, VA 22314; Phone: (703) 684-7710.

Online sites

www.teenshealth.org/teen/index2.html
Useful information and general mental-health advice.

pbskids.org/itsmylife
Web site dealing with issues surrounding daily life. Whatever problem you're dealing with, other kids and teens have gone through the same thing.

www.kidshealth.org
General mental-health information.

www.child.net
The largest nonprofit resource of any kind on the Internet, with more than forty-five national and regional children's and teens' resource and activity sites. Links to six thousand other resources, including more than seven hundred public libraries, school districts, and individual school web sites.

www.aacap.org/
American Academy of Child and Adolescent Psychiatry web site.

www.teenadviceonline.org/
If you're looking for advice, you can submit a question to Teen Advice Online. A volunteer advisor, age thirteen or older, will provide suggestions for your problem, then you make your decision.

www.nostigma.org/hope.html
Official site of The National Mental Health Awareness Campaign to fight stigma about mental illness. Get free information, share your own story, and learn ways you can raise awareness in your school and community.

teenink.com/

Read what other kids are writing about or submit your own story. Teens write about health issues—articles dealing with injuries, drugs, eating disorders, illness, smoking, cancer, anorexia, depression, suicide, facing the death of a loved one, and much more. Prose and poetry all written by teens.

Hot lines and help lines

Talk to someone, ask a question, or find a referral at any of the following:

Teen Advice

teenadvice.about.com/

This About.com Guide to Teen Advice offers selective lists of web links in a number of subject areas such as peer advice, medical advice, expert advice, help lines, violence tip lines, talking to parents, girl stuff, and guy stuff. There are also online discussion forums and regular articles on a variety of teen topics.

AL-ANON/ALATEEN (For friends and family of people who have a drinking problem.)
800-344-2666

Nine Line: 800-999-9999

Youth depression hot line: 800-HIT-HOME

Bulimia/anorexia disorders: 800-227-4785

Peer violence hot line: 877-REPORT-IT

Abuse, rape, and incest hot line: 800-656-HOPE

National suicide hot line: 800-SUICIDE

Index

About the Author

Gerri C. Borenstein has always wanted to write books for young adults. From her earliest scribbles and poems to her present career as a freelance writer, Gerri has tried to educate and empower people with her work. Her career began as a copywriter for several advertising and marketing firms around Boston, Massachusetts. From there, she moved to upstate New York where she wrote radio commercials, newsletters, and short stories. She was the creator of Kidscope™, the Horoscope for Kids; writer of a humor column; and most recently a contributing editor for the latest edition of *Alternative Medicine: The Definitive Guide.* Gerri has a bachelor of arts degree in philosophy and a master of science degree in communications from Boston University. She lives in Clinton, New York, with her husband and her two children.

Acknowledgements

Writing this book put me in touch with a number of people—including friends and family—who generously shared their experiences, opinions, and ideas with me. Special thanks to my husband, Neal, for guiding me with his medical expertise in the field of psychiatry and for editing my work with his usual care and good humor; the following mental health practitioners, teachers, and parents for their candor: Phyllis DiLea, CSWR, ACSW, Thomas Scott, Ph.D., Judith Logue, Ph.D., Madge Flynn, Ph.D., Donna Elefante, Daniel DeStefano, M.D., Cara Gondek, and Gail Vivyan; and to my editor, Meredith DeSousa, and all the people at Scholastic for tackling these sensitive subjects in the Life Balance series.